Island Style!
A Kid's Guide To Coronado, California

Photography By John D. Weigand
Poetry By Penelope Dyan

Bellissima Publishing, LLC
Jamul, California
www.bellissimapublishing.com

Copyright © 2013 by Penny D. Weigand and John D. Weigand

All rights reserved. No part of this book may be
reproduced or transmitted in any form or by any means,
electronic or mechanical, including photocopying,
recording, or by any other means, or by any information or
storage retrieval system, without permission from the publisher.

ISBN 978-1-61477-090-9
First Edition

"Fortune brings in some boats that are not steered."

WILLIAM SHAKESPEARE

Island Style!
Bellissima Publishing, LLC

Introduction

Across the Coronado Bridge from San Diego is the sleepy, step back into the past, small town or Coronado. The locals say they are Islanders, even though they live on a peninsula; and a bicycle is a common mode of transportation for many of the locals. You can find everything you need here, and locals never like to leave their "Island" even though they are actually connected by a land bridge on the far side that takes them down the Silver Strand Beach to what is called the South Bay area. Naturally, this is a great place for kids, with lots of fun shopping, as well as great restaurants, parks and beaches, not to mention the world famous Hotel Del Coronado where Marilyn Monroe shot the movie, "Some Like It Hot!" with Jack Lemmon and Tony Curtis, a movie some parents may remember as a piece of Hollywood history! And the magic of Hollywood (by the way) is just up the coast of California, .past Disneyland, and not too far from Coronado!

Written by award winning author, attorney and former teacher, Penelope Dyan, with rhyme and word recognition techniques, kids and practice reading skills as they learn about this great place. There is also a fun music video on the Bellissimavideo YouTube Channel that goes along with this book. This is a book for kids that has an educational purpose and that will look great on your coffee table!

Island Style!
Bellissima Publishing, LLC

Island Style!
A Kid's Guide To Coronado, California

Photography By John D. Weigand
Poetry By Penelope Dyan

From San Diego, California
over the Coronado bridge
you can take your car.
Because from San Diego,
it is NOT very far.

If you like, you can take a ferry boat
to and from this beautiful place.
Then (if you choose) you can walk
through the town
at your own leisurely pace.

Coronado is so close to San Diego, that you can see the city of San Diego from the Ferry Boat Landing's shore; but please pay attention, because there's EVEN more!

There is a sign above you
that leads the way,
to this glorious little Island
where you can shop, laugh, eat,
stay and play.

The restaurants and shops
are the first things you see.
Peeking out from behind bushes,
plants, trees and flowers,
is where THEY will be!

Here is something fun
the whole family can do,
because you can ride a bicycle car
built for FOUR (or more) not two!

And then you can go to
beautiful Central Beach.
It isn't VERY far to reach.
you can squish your toes
in the nice warm sand,
and you can watch
as the waves lap against the land.

And if you forgot your swimsuit,
and you want to swim,
you can buy another swimsuit,
at Dale's Swim Shop, just walk in!
Dale's is a friendly place.
A smile ALWAYS greets your face!
You will shop here if you are wise,
Dale ALWAYS has a good price.
She is ALWAYS helpful,
and she ALWAYS has your size!

Upon a swing you can glide and fly.
Perhaps you'll EVEN reach the sky!

Then you can slip right down this slide!
From the fun of Coronado
You just can't hide!
Even if you want to be a grumpy bear,
you'll find fun just everywhere!

As you wheel around
you might want to make a stop.
at this little place,
the Island Surf Shop!
And here you can purchase
enough fun beach gear,
and it will last you year after year!

Finally, you all decide
to put your feet to the metal,
and to the Hotel Coronado
you decide to pedal.
Mom says tonight here you'll stay,
and THAT night...
as in your hotel bed you lay...
you imagine the mermaids in the sea.
There is NO other place that
YOU'D rather be!
And as at the ceiling you stare and stare,
through the window stars are sparkling!
They are just EVERYWHERE!

"If I could reach up and hold a star for every time you've made me smile, the entire evening sky would be in the palm of my hand."

AUTHOR UNKNOWN

www.ingramcontent.com/pod-product-compliance
Ingram Content Group UK Ltd.
Pitfield, Milton Keynes, MK11 3LW, UK
UKHW060133240426
12048UKWH00002B/21